South Dakota'

This book is dedicated to the best dog that ever lived. Terrapin.

Rest in peace T. Love you forever.

— Rebecca Lynch

Table Of Contents

South Dakota's Haunting Shadows

Introduction:

In the wake of his remarkable journey through the haunted tales of "Louisiana's Ghostly Gumbo," Max found himself standing at a crossroads of excitement and uncertainty. The old journal had transported him from being a mere reader to an active participant in supernatural adventures, revealing the chilling mysteries that lay hidden within the states of America. With every chapter, he had encountered spectral entities, explored haunted landmarks, and connected with the spirits of the past.

Yet, as Max bid farewell to his dear friend Marie, he knew that his spectral odyssey was far from over. The journal, still imbued with a mysterious power, beckoned him to the next state in the series, "South Dakota's Haunting Shadows." Louisiana had revealed its secrets, but now he stood at the threshold of a new state, ready to embrace its haunting mysteries.

With a heart filled with wonder and a spirit emboldened by his experiences, Max set his sights on South Dakota, a land steeped in history and shrouded in mystery. His mind swirled with images of Mount Rushmore's majestic visages, the eerie whispers of Sica Hollow, and the spectral guests of Hotel Alex Johnson. The words from the last page of the Louisiana journal echoed in his mind, "Welcome to The Rushmore State," urging him to delve deeper into the chilling stories that awaited him.

The journey ahead promised not just spectral encounters, but the chance to uncover forgotten tales of the past and forge new friendships. Max knew that The Rushmore State had many secrets to reveal, and he was determined to unlock them one by one. With every chapter, he would uncover the haunted shadows that lurked beneath the surface, connecting the living and the departed in a dance of mystery and intrigue.

As Max stepped onto the pages of "South Dakota's Haunting Shadows," he couldn't help but feel a sense of awe and trepidation. The journal had become more than just a book; it was a gateway to adventure, where history intertwined with the supernatural, and where every turn of the page revealed a new mystery to unravel.

With his trusted journal in hand and a heart brimming with curiosity, Max set forth on his next supernatural odyssey, ready to embrace the chilling mysteries of The Rushmore State. South Dakota awaited him, and he was determined to discover its haunting secrets, one spectral shadow at a time.

"THE HAUNTING OF CORBEY HALL"

On a warm summer evening, as the sun dipped below the horizon, twelve-year-old Max stood in awe before the grand entrance of Mount Marty University in South Dakota. The ancient stone walls seemed to carry secrets from long ago, their faint mossy scent whispering stories of the past. His heart beat fast with excitement and a touch of nervousness as his fingers grazed the rough bricks.

Beside him stood Bryson, his twelve-year-old cousin. With his curly dark hair, glasses, and dreams of becoming a pastor, Bryson was a steady presence. Their loyal dog, Terrapin, wagged her tail, sensing adventure in the air.

Max had come to South Dakota to visit his relatives, and Bryson was his closest cousin and friend. Intrigued by rumors of the eerie tales connected to Mount Marty, they were both eager to uncover the truth.

As they roamed the campus, they met Professor Rutten, a man in his forties with red hair and a beard, known for his knowledge of the school's ghostly history. When Max and Bryson asked about the stories, Professor Rutten's eyes lit up.

"Hello, young explorers," he greeted them, leading them to a quiet corner. "Mount Marty University holds quite a few ghostly legends. One of the most spine-tingling involves Corbey Hall. A long time ago, a girl entered an elevator and vanished without a trace."

Bryson's eyes widened, and Max felt a shiver ripple down his spine. "Vanished? What happened to her?"

With a solemn nod, Professor Rutten began, "No one truly knows. Some say she disappeared like a wisp of smoke, while others think she crossed into another world. But what remains certain is her lingering presence and the waves of sadness felt around the elevators."

As day gave way to night, the three found themselves near Corbey Hall. The dimly lit elevator beckoned to them, and a chill ran down Max's spine as they stepped inside. The air smelled of ancient wood, and Max traced his fingers over the cool metal railing.

Suddenly, the lights flickered and faded, plunging them into darkness.

Max's heart raced as Bryson's hand clutched his tightly. In the pitch-black, they heard faint sounds of buttons being pressed, and the elevator began to ascend, stopping on each floor. Yet, no one else shared the ride with them.

Terrapin growled softly, her senses attuned to the eerie atmosphere. Max struggled to stay calm, but his heart pounded with each passing floor.

Then, buttons started lighting up on their own, as if pressed by invisible hands. The elevator moved as if guided by some unseen force, taking them to floors they hadn't chosen.

Bryson's voice trembled, "Max, did you touch any buttons?"

Max shook his head, his voice lost in the grip of fear. An eerie realization settled in – something otherworldly was at play.

The elevator finally stopped, its doors sliding open to reveal a corridor shrouded in darkness. They hurried out, and the lights blinked back to life.

"Let's get out of here," Max whispered, his words barely audible.

As they left the unsettling hallways of Mount Marty, unease lingered. The supernatural encounters they had just experienced were unlike anything they had known. Guided by Professor Rutten's chilling tales and their own curiosity, they understood that South Dakota's past held many more secrets.

With each step, Max and Bryson were resolute in unraveling those mysteries. Their hearts, a blend of curiosity and unease, drove them forward. As cousins and friends, they embraced their journey into The Rushmore State's enigmatic history, accompanied by Terrapin's unwavering companionship. With every new discovery and every spectral whisper, they bridged the gap between the present and the past.

And as they listened to stories of St. Benedict and the university's teachings, Bryson couldn't help but envision himself returning to Mount Marty someday. The teachings seemed to fit perfectly with his dream of becoming a pastor. The echoes of the past and the shadows of ghosts were now woven into his own story, a tale waiting to be written.

"Larry's Standing Ovation"

In the heart of Sioux Falls, South Dakota, the grand Orpheum Theatre stood as a silent witness to a bygone era of captivating performances. Max and Bryson found themselves drawn to its enchanting allure, eager to uncover the mysteries that swirled within its historic walls. Terrapin, their loyal and gentle golden doodle, wagged her tail in excitement, sensing the curiosity that filled the air.

As they entered the opulent theater, the soft scent of old, polished wood embraced them, intermingled with the aroma of freshly popped popcorn. The grand chandeliers shimmered overhead, casting a warm glow on the ornate ceilings and velvety curtains that adorned the stage.

"Wow, this place is amazing!" Bryson exclaimed, his eyes wide with wonder.

"It's like stepping back in time," Max agreed, captivated by the theater's timeless beauty.

The boys wandered further into the theater, the echoes of their footsteps blending with the faint whispers of a ghostly presence. Max could feel the mysterious ghost's yearning for the spotlight, the lingering desire for an encore that eluded him in life.

"There's something about this theater that feels so alive," Bryson mused, his eyes scanning the vast expanse of the auditorium.

Just then, a soft, haunting melody filled the air, causing Max and Bryson to exchange intrigued glances. It seemed to emanate from the stage, drawing them closer with its magnetic allure.

Terrapin's ears perked up, and she let out a low, mournful howl that harmonized with the spectral music, as if joining in a ghostly bravo.

"Did you hear that?" Max asked, his voice tinged with awe.

"I think Terrapin is giving her own applause," Bryson chuckled, patting the loyal canine on the head.

As the boys approached the stage, they noticed something unusual - a faint glow coming from a hidden corner behind the curtains. It seemed to pull them closer, as if an unseen force was guiding their steps.

Terrapin, too, seemed drawn to the spot, her tail wagging with excitement as he led the way. Max and Bryson followed, their curiosity piqued.

Behind the stage, they found an old, weathered wall with the name "Larry" elegantly written in cursive letters. It was faint, as if time had gently faded the ink, but the name was unmistakable.

"Larry..." Max whispered, his heart quickening with emotion.

"He must have written his name here when he was a performer," Bryson said, awe evident in his voice.

As they stood before Larry's name, the theater seemed to come alive with energy. The soft glow of the ghostly lights danced around them, and a warm breeze swept through the stage.

"I think he wants us to remember him," Max said, feeling a deep connection to the mysterious ghost.

"He's waiting for his encore," Bryson added, a mix of admiration and sadness in his voice.

Terrapin nudged against them, as if affirming the significance of the moment.

Max and Bryson exchanged a knowing look, understanding that they had the power to give Larry the encore he had longed for all these years. With a sense of reverence, they placed their hands on the wall, as if connecting with the spirit of the departed performer.

"Larry, you were an incredible performer," Max said, his voice filled with sincerity. "You deserve your standing ovation."

"We won't forget you," Bryson added, his eyes shining with determination. "Your name will live on in this theater and in our hearts."

As if in response, the theater's lights flickered in a spectral dance, and the soft melody filled the air once more. Max and Bryson joined in, clapping their hands in rhythm with the ghostly music.

"Bravo, Larry!" they called out, their voices carrying through the auditorium.

"You were amazing!" Max added, a sense of reverence in his tone.

Larry's ghostly form seemed to shimmer and brighten, as if filled with newfound joy. The theater pulsed with energy, as if the unseen audience was joining in the standing ovation.

As the applause and howls subsided, Larry's ghostly form glowed even brighter. With a radiant smile, he turned to Max and Bryson, his eyes filled with gratitude and peace.

"Thank you," Larry whispered, his voice barely audible but filled with heartfelt appreciation.

As the boys left the Orpheum Theatre, they knew that they had been a part of something extraordinary. They had given Larry the encore he had longed for, allowing him to pass on to a realm of eternal rest.

"He truly loved the stage," Max said, moved by the passion that radiated from the spectral performer.

"And he'll never be forgotten," Bryson replied, knowing that Larry's spirit would live on in the memories of those who witnessed his spectral performance.

With Terrapin's gentle presence and the bond of their friendship, they knew they were ready to face whatever chilling mysteries The Rushmore State had to offer. The echoes of the Orpheum Theatre's haunting melodies lingered in their hearts, guiding them to the next spectral encounter that awaited them in their supernatural odyssey.

"Echoes of the Gulch"

Max, Bryson, and Terrapin embarked on an enthralling journey through the eerie shadows of South Dakota, and their next destination was the breathtaking Devil's Gulch. The quartzite cliffs soared above them, and the tranquility of the landscape stood in stark contrast to the legends that cloaked this place.

Terrapin, ever vigilant, led the way, her paws rustling through the fallen leaves on the trail. The boys followed, anticipation building with each step, and the crisp sound of leaves crunching beneath their feet added a touch of autumnal charm to their adventure. They had heard the folklore surrounding Jesse James' daring escape, but the historical accuracy of the leap remained shrouded in doubt.

In September of 1876, Jesse James and his notorious gang were on the run after committing one of the most infamous bank robberies in American history. The daring heist took place in Northfield, Minnesota, where the outlaws brazenly held up the First National Bank. The robbery turned into a disastrous shootout, leaving several gang members dead and wounded. The law was catching up to them, and Jesse faced a choice – jump the 18-foot-wide Devil's Gulch or take his chances with the relentless posse on their trail.

Legend has it that with lawmen closing in, Jesse gritted his teeth and urged his stolen horse to take the leap. Miraculously, they cleared the daunting gorge, evading capture and escaping into the dust of history. The story of Jesse James' leap has since become a fascinating part of South Dakota folklore, drawing visitors from all over who come to Devil's Gulch to witness the place where the notorious outlaw made his daring escape.

As they explored the area, the refreshing scent of autumn lingered in the air, invigorating their senses. They noticed something peculiar in the dirt below the gulch. Picking up a handful, they discovered old coins glimmering in the sunlight. Bryson's eyes widened in surprise. "Look, Max! Ancient coins hidden in the dirt."

Max examined the coins closely, marveling at their aged appearance. "These must have been here for generations. Maybe even from Jesse James' time."

Terrapin sniffed at the ground, and as they turned their attention back to the gulch, they were startled by a sudden scent of worn leather that filled the air. The earthy aroma seemed to materialize out of thin air, leaving them bewildered.

"What was that?" Bryson asked, his eyes darting around.

Max's heart raced as he glanced at Terrapin, who was now wagging her tail excitedly. "I think we're about to find out."

The sound of approaching hooves grew louder, echoing through the gulch, and a shimmering apparition appeared before them. There, in the ethereal light, was the ghostly figure of Jesse James himself, astride his horse, reenacting that fateful leap across Devil's Gulch.

The boys gasped in astonishment, their eyes fixed on the mesmerizing spectacle before them. Jesse's eyes met theirs, and a silent understanding passed between them. It was as if the ghostly figure was acknowledging their presence, even in death.

"He did it, Bryson! He really did," Max whispered, filled with awe.

As the ghostly reenactment waned, the boys were left with a mix of wonder and skepticism. They had borne witness to a piece of folklore brought to life, yet the mystery surrounding the leap persisted. The encounter had left an indelible mark on their hearts, and they knew that their quest to unravel South Dakota's mysterious tales would be filled with more spectral surprises.

In the fading light, the ghostly presence spoke to them in a whisper carried by the rustling leaves. It was a soft, haunting voice, a plea from the other side. "Tell them I made it... Tell them I did cross the gulch."

Max and Bryson nodded, promising to share the truth with the world. Terrapin seemed to sense the solemnity of the moment, as if she, too, understood the significance of the encounter.

As the sun dipped below the horizon, casting an ethereal glow over Devil's Gulch, Max, Bryson, and Terrapin pressed on. The adventure was only just beginning, and with each chapter, they would delve deeper into the haunting secrets of The Rushmore State, guided by their unyielding curiosity and the steadfast loyalty of their canine companion.

In the spirit of Jesse James' enduring escape, they vowed to explore the truth behind the legends and preserve the memory of those who had ventured into the unknown. The sound of leaves crunching beneath their feet and the autumnal scent in the air would forever remind them of the day they encountered the ghostly leap of Jesse James and embraced the mysteries that The Rushmore State had in store for them.

"MURAL SECRETS OF THE CORN PALACE"

In the heart of Mitchell, South Dakota, stood an iconic structure known as the Corn Palace. Every year, locals and tourists gather to witness its grandeur, adorned with murals crafted entirely from corn. Yet, beneath its festive exterior, there lay a history veiled in mystery and whispers of the past.

Max and Bryson's journey led them to this unique landmark, guided by Terrapin, their loyal four-legged companion. As they approached the Corn Palace, the boys felt a sense of anticipation mingled with the scent of freshly harvested cornfields nearby. It was autumn, and the air carried the crispness of the changing season.

"The Corn Palace looks like an 'amaizing' place," Bryson quipped with a grin, earning a chuckle from Max.

"Indeed, it does," Max replied, sharing in Bryson's humor. "Let's see if it lives up to its name."

The Corn Palace had witnessed many events throughout its history, from festive celebrations to solemn gatherings. Locals shared tales of how, during the Great Depression, the Corn Palace served as a beacon of hope and resilience, inspiring the community with its vibrant murals.

As Max, Bryson, and Terrapin explored the palace's interior, they sensed an inexplicable energy that seemed to echo with the voices of the past. They wandered through the halls adorned with corn mosaics, each telling a unique story. Max's fingers brushed against the rough texture of the corn, almost as if the mural itself yearned to share its secrets.

While studying a particularly striking mural depicting an ancient tribe's harvest festival, the boys heard faint whispers carried on the wind. They exchanged curious glances, drawn to the source of the ethereal voices.

As they moved deeper into the Corn Palace, the voices grew clearer, weaving tales of the past into their surroundings. It was as if the spirits of those who once walked these halls had returned to share their stories. The boys listened in awe as the past unfurled before them.

Among the whispers, they caught fragments of a story about a legendary artist named Oscar Howe. A Yanktonai Dakota from South Dakota, Howe had left a profound impact on contemporary Native American art, paving the way for future artists. His bold casein and tempera paintings were marked by bright colors, dynamic motion, and pristine lines - a reflection of his heritage and vision.

Terrapin, ever vigilant, seemed to react to the spirits' presence, her ears perking up and her tail wagging in acknowledgment. She, too, sensed the echoes of the past surrounding them.

As they explored further, Max and Bryson found themselves inexplicably drawn to a hidden corner of the Corn Palace. There, obscured by the passage of time, they discovered an old sketchbook bearing Oscar Howe's name. The pages of the sketchbook revealed the artist's intimate thoughts and aspirations, a window into the creative process behind the murals.

Deep in contemplation, Max and Bryson felt an overwhelming urge to add their own creations to the sketchbook. They sketched their own visions, intertwining them with Howe's original drawings. It was as if their drawings breathed new life into the past, connecting the present with the history that resided within the walls of the Corn Palace.

As the boys completed their sketches, an astonishing sight unfolded before their eyes. The murals on the walls seemed to come alive with an otherworldly glow, the figures dancing and the scenes pulsating with life. Max and Bryson stood in awe as their additions seamlessly merged with the existing artwork, as if the spirits of the past were acknowledging their contributions.

The whispers of the past grew stronger, resonating with gratitude and joy. It was as if the spirits were applauding their young visitors for their reverence and creativity.

Before leaving, Max and Bryson felt compelled to express their gratitude for the privilege of hearing these forgotten tales. In unison, they promised to honor and share the stories they had encountered, ensuring that the voices of the past would not fade away.

With hearts full of wonder and reverence, they bid farewell to the Corn Palace, their minds teeming with visions of its vibrant history. Max and Bryson knew that their adventure had only just begun, and the echoes of the past would continue to guide them as they delved deeper into the mysteries of South Dakota's haunting shadows. And as they stepped outside, a sense of accomplishment and camaraderie filled the air – for they now carried a part of Oscar Howe's enchantment with them, forever intertwined with their own story.

"Whispers of Ancient Warriors"

As Max, Bryson, and Terrapin journeyed northward to Sisseton, South Dakota, they knew they were stepping into a world steeped in Native American mystique. The city of Sisseton, bearing the name of the Sisseton Sioux, and the legendary Sica Hollow State Park beckoned them with its mysterious tales of creation and vengeance.

As the sun dipped below the horizon, casting eerie shadows across the forested ravines, the boys arrived at the entrance of Sica Hollow. The air was charged with an electrifying blend of anticipation and unease. Bryson couldn't resist a shiver running down his spine, while Max's heart pounded with excitement and apprehension.

Legend whispered that this sacred place was once feared as "Sica," the embodiment of evil. The Dakota Sioux, who hunted these lands, believed supernatural forces dwelled here, weaving tales of warriors and spirits. The boys sensed the weight of history and the thrill of the unknown as they ventured deeper into the heart of Sica Hollow.

Terrapin led the way, her senses attuned to the ancient spirits that supposedly roamed the woods. The sounds of leaves crunching beneath their feet seemed to echo louder, magnifying the feeling that they were not alone.

As twilight gave way to darkness, the forest transformed into an eerie realm of shadows and whispers. The boys could see how, in the flickering moonlight, the ordinary could become extraordinary, and every rustle of leaves or hoot of an owl could be mistaken for something otherworldly.

Unfazed by the chilling tales, Terrapin pressed on, urging them forward. They came across the reddish bogs that held the legends of ancestral blood and flesh, and the boys couldn't help but imagine the ancient ceremonies that once unfolded on this very soil.

With each step, the air seemed to thicken with a sense of history, and the trail they followed appeared like a spectral path leading to the unknown. The gurgling of the bogs took on an ethereal quality, as if they were witnessing a ritual from another time.

As they ventured deeper into the heart of Sica Hollow, the boys heard faint echoes of cries and war whoops, haunting remnants of an ancient battle. A chill ran down Max's spine, and Bryson's heart raced with adrenaline.

Terrapin let out a low growl, sensing the presence of unseen spirits. But amidst the eeriness, the boys felt a strange sense of comfort. It was as if the spirits were communicating with them, sharing stories of bravery and honor from ages past.

Bryson's voice quivered with excitement as he said, "This place is brimming with history and mystery! It's like we're part of something ancient and powerful."

Max agreed, feeling a profound connection to the land and its legends. "We may not see them, but their presence is all around us," he replied.

Their adventure in Sica Hollow led them to a quiet spot where the forest canopy above created an otherworldly ambience. Max and Bryson sat down, their hearts pounding in sync with the rhythm of the forest.

In the darkness, they felt an inexplicable warmth and reassurance. The spirits seemed to acknowledge their reverence for the land and its history, embracing them like old friends from a bygone era.

As the night wore on, the boys exchanged stories and laughter, knowing they were not alone. Terrapin, ever the loyal companion, wagged her tail in approval, as if she too sensed the sacredness of the moment.

As the first rays of sunlight gently broke through the forest canopy, Terrapin began to dig at the base of an ancient tree. Her keen senses had led her to a hidden treasure buried beneath the earth. Max and Bryson watched with curiosity as she carefully unearthed an old, weathered arrowhead.

Max picked up the arrowhead, its smooth surface now roughened by the passage of time. He held it in his hand, feeling the weight of history within its delicate frame. A sense of reverence washed over him as he realized the significance of this discovery – a connection to the land and its native heritage.

"This arrowhead is a piece of Sica Hollow's story," Max said, his voice filled with awe. "I'll keep it close, as a reminder of the mysteries we encountered and the respect we have for the Native American culture."

Bryson nodded, understanding the importance of the find. "It's like a token of friendship from the spirits of this place," he remarked. "A symbol of the bond we formed with Sica Hollow."

Terrapin, seemingly satisfied with her discovery, wagged her tail as if in agreement. Max carefully placed the arrowhead in his pocket, knowing that it would forever remind him of the sacredness of this land and the ancient stories it held.

As they bid farewell to Sica Hollow, the boys carried with them not only memories of their thrilling encounters but also a newfound appreciation for the rich heritage of the Dakota Sioux. Their journey through South Dakota's haunting shadows had deepened their understanding of the land's history and the spirits that dwelled within it.

With the arrowhead close to his heart, Max knew that he would never forget the mystical allure of Sica Hollow and the respect he felt for the Native American culture that had thrived there for generations.

As the sun rose higher in the sky, casting a golden glow over the landscape, Max, Bryson, and Terrapin continued their quest through South Dakota's mysterious corners. The mysteries were far from over, and with each step, they embraced the wonder and excitement of the unknown.

For in the heart of this ancient land, they had found not just spectral tales and chilling encounters, but also a profound appreciation for the rich tapestry of history that had shaped the state of South Dakota. And with their hearts open to the magic that surrounded them, they journeyed forth, ready to unravel more whispers of the past and forge new bonds with the spirits that guarded the secrets of the land.

"There's No Place Like Home"

Tucked away in the quiet corners of Aberdeen, South Dakota, stood the mysterious Easton Castle, a historical treasure shrouded in whispers and intrigue. Max and Bryson, accompanied by their trusty companion, Terrapin, ventured forth to explore the secrets of this mysterious place. Little did they know that the castle's connection to the world of Oz would lead them down a haunting path of eerie enchantment.

As they arrived at The Easton Castle, raindrops danced on the windows, lending an air of mystery to their adventure. The weather seemed to mirror the feelings in their hearts—unsettled yet undeterred.

Tandy Holman, the current owner, welcomed them with a warm smile and invited them inside. The boys listened intently as she shared tales of L. Frank Baum's visits and the strange events that had occurred over the years. "Legend has it," Tandy whispered, "that the yellow bricks were taken from the Wizard of Oz movie set in 1939, and since then, they've been said to be haunted."

Max and Bryson exchanged uneasy glances as they learned that visitors to the castle had reported eerie sightings and unexplained noises. They couldn't help but feel a mixture of curiosity and fear as they wondered what secrets the haunted yellow bricks might hold.

When the rain subsided, they ventured outside to see the yellow bricks that adorned the castle's exterior. The sun peeked through the clouds, and a beautiful rainbow arched across the sky, adding an ethereal glow to the scene.

As they admired the vibrant colors, a faint melody filled the air. The boys strained their ears, and to their astonishment, they could hear the soft, haunting notes of "Somewhere Over the Rainbow" by Judy Garland. The song seemed to be carried on the breeze, as if the spirits of Oz were whispering the familiar tune.

Terrapin, usually a cheerful and adventurous spirit, appeared on edge, her tail tucked, and ears perked, sensing the presence of something otherworldly. The boys found comfort in her presence but couldn't ignore the unsettling atmosphere that surrounded them.

With caution, they returned to the castle's interior, where Tandy continued to share tales of hauntings and unexplained phenomena. The yellow bricks that adorned the walls now seemed to shimmer with an unsettling energy, as if the spirits of Oz were trying to communicate through them.

In one of the grand chambers, Max and Bryson spotted an old gramophone, its horn tarnished with age. They hesitated for a moment before setting the needle on a dusty record. The melody of "Somewhere Over the Rainbow" filled the room once more, the haunting tune echoing off the walls.

The haunting melody seemed to grow louder, blending with the eerie moans that filled the air. The castle seemed to come alive with a cacophony of chilling sounds.

Just then, shadows began to dance along the walls, taking the form of familiar characters from Oz—the Scarecrow, the Tin Man, and the Lion. Their spectral figures moved with a desperate urgency, searching for "home" as there is no place like it. But the yellow brick road, broken and repurposed to build the castle, left them stranded, unable to find their way back.

During the haunting spectacle, a small shadow darted across the floor—it was Toto, the little dog that had been Dorothy's faithful companion in Oz. His presence brought both comfort and melancholy, reminding Max and Bryson of the enduring bond between Dorothy and her beloved pet.

As the haunting manifestations gradually subsided, Max and Bryson realized that the spirits of Oz were forever trapped within the yellow bricks, unable to find the home they so desperately sought. The boys couldn't help but feel a deep sense of empathy for these spectral figures, forever lost in a place not their own.

With a mixture of excitement and unease, the boys vowed to return someday to uncover more of The Easton Castle's chilling mysteries. As they stepped into the night, the rainbow still faintly visible in the distance, they couldn't help but feel that they had glimpsed a world beyond imagination—a realm where the fantastical and the haunted intertwined.

As they journeyed on, Max and Bryson felt a mix of exhilaration and uneasiness, carrying with them the lingering echoes of the haunted yellow bricks and the mysterious spirits of Oz. They stepped into the awaiting car, and just as they were about to drive away, the haunting melody of "Somewhere Over the Rainbow" came on the radio, filling the air with an eerie yet mesmerizing tune. It was as if the spirits of The Easton Castle were bidding them farewell, their presence lingering in the echoes of the song. With a sense of wonder and curiosity, they set off towards their next destination, carrying with them the mysteries and enchantments they had encountered, forever intertwined with the whispers of haunted Oz.

"Buried Bones"

LaFramboise Island, nestled amidst the Missouri River near Pierre, South Dakota's capital, held a mysterious allure that intrigued Max, Bryson, and Terrapin as they set foot on its remote shores. Whispers of strange happenings and ghostly apparitions swirled around the island, but their sense of adventure overpowered any fear they might have felt.

As they ventured along the island's meandering trails, the sun began to set, casting a golden hue upon the landscape. The fading light painted the island, known for its lush cottonwood trees, in surreal colors, adding an ethereal quality to their surroundings. The boys marveled at the beauty of nature around them, finding peace amid the haunting ambiance.

At dusk, they spotted a figure in the distance –
a young boy standing alone near the
riverbank, where cottonwood fluff floated
gently in the breeze. His presence seemed
both melancholic and intriguing, and without
a word, he beckoned them to follow. Curiosity
and fascination drove them to trail behind him
as he led them deeper into the island's heart.

The forest grew thicker and more foreboding
with each step, yet they felt an inexplicable
connection to the spirit of the place. Terrapin's
ears perked up, sensing something beyond
their understanding. As they continued, the
island seemed to come alive with whispers
and sighs, as if the spirits of the past were
awakening to share their untold stories.

The ghostly boy led them deeper into the
heart of LaFramboise Island, and as they
walked, Terrapin, their loyal companion,
seemed particularly alert, her nose sniffing the
air with determination.

"That must be the ghost boy that people say leads them into the woods and disappears," Bryson whispered to Max, his voice barely above a murmur. "But it's strange, he seems like he's looking for something."

Max nodded, intrigued by the mysterious boy's behavior. "You're right. Maybe he needs our help to find whatever he's searching for."

As they followed the ghostly figure, the trees cast eerie shadows, adding to the mysterious atmosphere. The air was thick with an inexplicable energy, and the sounds of rustling leaves seemed to echo with whispers of the past.

The ghost boy turned to face them, his eyes filled with a mix of sadness and gratitude. Before Max and Bryson could utter another word, he smiled faintly and vanished into thin air, leaving them with a sense of wonder and bewilderment.

"What just happened?" Max wondered aloud, trying to make sense of the ghostly encounter.

Bryson shook his head in awe. "I don't know, but he seemed like he needed something from us."

As they continued exploring, Terrapin's keen senses led her to a mysterious spot in the underbrush. The boys watched in amazement as she began to dig with fervor. After some time, she uncovered a pile of old bones, centuries-old remnants buried deep beneath the earth.

"They're not human bones... They look like they're hundreds of years old," Bryson said, examining the bones closely.

Max's eyes widened with realization. "They're dog bones."

Terrapin had found something significant – the remains of a dog that had long been lost on the island. Max's heart skipped a beat as he realized what this meant. Terrapin had discovered the ghost boy's long-lost dog, the faithful companion he had searched for all these years.

"It's his dog," Max whispered, touched by the discovery. "The ghost boy was leading us into the forest to help him find his missing dog."

A sense of compassion washed over Max and Bryson as they understood the ghost boy's plea for help. He had been searching for his beloved companion, unable to rest until they were reunited.

With newfound determination, Max held up the dog's old bones and showed them to the ghost boy. In that moment, something extraordinary happened. The spirit of the lost dog emerged from the depths of the hole, shimmering with a warm, ethereal light. The ghost boy's eyes lit up with joy and recognition as he extended his arms, and the spirit of the dog jumped into his embrace.

As the ghost boy held his long-lost friend, a sense of peace and contentment washed over them. The bond between the boy and his dog was undeniable, transcending time and death itself.

With a final smile of gratitude, the ghost boy and his dog faded away into the night, their spirits finally at peace. Max, Bryson, and Terrapin stood in awe, having witnessed a tale of love and loyalty that defied the boundaries of the mortal world.

Their hearts filled with a mixture of sadness and joy, they knew that LaFramboise Island held more secrets than they could ever comprehend. The ancient spirits that dwelled there would forever remain a mystery, but they had experienced something extraordinary – a world where love and devotion endured beyond the veil of death.

With Terrapin curled up contentedly in the backseat, they drove off, ready to embrace the next mysterious chapter awaiting them in the great Black Hills, where new adventures and wonders would surely unfold.

"WHAT IS BEHIND DOOR 807?"

Amidst the heart of Rapid City, South Dakota, loomed the historic Alex Johnson Hotel, a monument to time's passage. Max, Bryson, and Terrapin found themselves drawn to its stories, ready to explore its intriguing past. The hotel stood as both a relic of bygone eras and a stage for spectral tales.

The hotel's exterior bore a regal charm, its secrets hidden within its walls. Among the tales whispered within its corridors was the haunting presence of the lady in white—a figure said to linger on the eighth floor, seeking her elusive groom who never materialized. Intrigued by the stories, the boys decided to embark on the hotel's ghost tour, eager to step into the footprints of history.

The tour unfolded like a dance through time's shadowy corridors, each step laced with echoes of lives long past. Climbing towards the eighth floor, anticipation hung thick in the air, a palpable energy that gripped Max and Bryson in its thrall. They exchanged knowing glances, both eager and apprehensive about what lay ahead.

The guide's voice was tinged with a tremor as they recounted the tale of the lady in white. Room 807, it seemed, was her realm—a place where love's promise had curdled into heartbreak. The boys listened intently, feeling the weight of a centuries-old tragedy hanging in the air.

Crossing the threshold of room 807, a shiver trailed down their spines. A delicate aroma—of fading roses and forgotten memories—swirled around them, almost tangible. The wallpaper's texture seemed to echo with whispers of lives lived within these walls, bridging past and present. Terrapin's ears perked, attuned to nuances of sound that transcended the ordinary.

The guide's words faded to a mere hum as the room's atmosphere enveloped them. In the moonlit embrace of the window, the lady in white stood—an ethereal figure draped in spectral fabric, her face veiled by an air of melancholy. Moonlight painted her form with a ghostly luminescence.

Max and Bryson stood, mesmerized by the apparition before them. The room's temperature plummeted, a sudden frigidity crept under their skin. The lady's mournful weeping echoed through the room, a sound that resonated deep within their souls.

As they watched, the room's ambiance shifted once more. A gust of wind brushed against their cheeks, carrying the scent of rain and distant lilies. The temperature dropped further, and the air seemed to crackle with a supernatural charge, making every hair on their skin stand on end.

Terrapin, usually unflappable, appeared entranced by the spectral presence. Her tail drooped, and a soft whimper escaped her lips, as if she sensed emotions that eluded the living. The lady in white's veil fluttered as if stirred by a breeze only she could feel, her figure radiating an otherworldly energy.

The room's boundaries blurred, a disorienting experience that melded past and present. The lady's gaze shifted, her mournful eyes meeting Max and Bryson's, carrying a sorrow that spanned centuries. They could almost feel the silkiness of her bridal attire and the cool touch of the glass against her fingertips.

A wave of empathy washed over the boys, their hearts connecting across the veil that separated them. The lady in white was a soul trapped in an endless quest, forever seeking the love that eluded her grasp. And in response to their unspoken understanding, her form began to wane, fading like mist.

Max and Bryson stood in a room that had reverted to its quiet stillness, the memory of the lady in white seared into their minds. Beyond the hotel's walls, the world carried on, oblivious to the ethereal encounter they had just shared. With Terrapin at their side, they stepped back into the realm of the living, their path stretching into South Dakota's mysteries.

Yet, as they moved forward, the memory of room 807 lingered—a poignant reminder of a love lost to time. Max and Bryson couldn't help but wish they could aid the lady in white in her eternal search, an impulse born from compassion. But as the hotel's corridors faded behind them, they carried with them the understanding that some mysteries were destined to remain unsolved.

With a determined spirit, they ventured forth, each step a testament to their connection with the mysterious past. The door closed behind them, a barrier between two worlds, and they embraced the journey that lay ahead —one filled with apparitions, echoes, and stories yet to unfold.

"Monumental Sorrow"

As the Fourth of July approached, an air of enchantment swept through the Black Hills, painting the landscape with anticipation. Max, Bryson, and Terrapin walked on a trail that wound its way up the mountain, the night scented with the earthy fragrance of pine and spruce. Above, stars twinkled like celestial gems, bestowing a touch of magic to the night.

Separating for a while, the boys walked their chosen paths, each drawn by the mysterious allure of the hidden door concealed behind Lincoln's formidable face. They approached the door together, and the door beckoned like a passage into the past, a doorway to a world forgotten—the Hall of Records. Stepping across the threshold, an intangible weight hung in the air, heavy with echoes of history.

Within the chamber, the atmosphere seemed to shift—an ethereal transformation that heralded the presence of a spectral figure. It was Gutzon Borglum, the visionary sculptor of Mount Rushmore, his form wispy and translucent. A sorrowful aura surrounded him, a manifestation of an artist who carried the weight of unfulfilled dreams. Trapped within these walls since his death, he was oblivious to the realization of his monumental vision.

Max's voice, a connection between the tangible and the spectral, resonated with empathy. "What shadows haunt you, Borglum? Your sculpture stands as a marvel that resonates with millions."

Bryson's words held a soothing quality as he observed the spectral form. "You chiseled magnificence into the stone. Why this lingering sorrow?"

Gutzon's spectral presence wavered, his voice a whisper from the past. "I dreamt of greatness beyond measure and I did not reach the pinnacle of my vision."

Max's response carried a comforting assurance. "Your work is etched into the hearts of generations. Yet, your spirit carries an anchor of unattained aspirations."

Bryson nodded, embracing the weight that Gutzon bore. "You yearned for more, Borglum, even though what you accomplished was monumental."

Gutzon's gaze drifted over the sculptures, his voice tinged with wistfulness. "I imagined the faces of Buffalo Bill Cody, Meriwether Lewis, William Clark, and Red Cloud gracing this stone canvas and I never got to finish it."

Bryson's words conveyed an understanding of Gutzon's grand aspirations. "Your visions held grandeur, Borglum, a tribute to the heroes of history."

Their words seemed to chip away at the spectral gloom, revealing a glint of light within. Gutzon's spirit appeared less burdened, a step closer to finding release.

"Why cradle this burden?" Max's question held a gentle persistence. "Your achievement is an exemplar for generations to come."

Bryson added, "Millions journey to witness your creation. Your legacy flourishes."

Gutzon's spectral form flickered, as if contemplating their words. Slowly, his essence brightened, the shroud of sorrow lifting like mist before dawn's light.

With a sense of surrender, Gutzon murmured, "Perhaps it is time to unshackle myself."

As the weight of his sorrow dissipated, the sky beyond burst into a radiant spectacle of fireworks. The pungent scent of gunpowder wafted in the air, mingling with the exhilaration of celebration.

Stepping out of the Hall of Records, Max, Bryson, and Terrapin were greeted by a sky ablaze with the splendor of color and light. In that moment, they felt a connection with Gutzon's spirit, as if his aspirations had finally been embraced by the brilliance of the world.

Gutzon's ghost lingered near the entrance, bathed in the cascade of colors overhead. A faint smile seemed to grace his lips, his essence finally unburdened. As the final firework illuminated the heavens, they sensed Gutzon's presence among the stars—a sculptor's spirit immortalized in the cosmic tapestry.

United, Max, Bryson, and Terrapin embraced the enchantment of the moment, celebrating not only a national treasure but also the spirit of an artist whose dreams continued to light the path for all who gazed upon his creation.

"THE GUARDIAN OF THE BULLOCK HOTEL"

Amid the storied streets of Deadwood in the Black Hills of South Dakota stood the Bullock Hotel, a testament to an era long past. Max, Bryson, and Terrapin ventured into its halls, sensing the whispers of history that clung to its walls. Seth Bullock, once the sheriff and builder of Deadwood, cast a spectral shadow upon the place, and as the boys explored, they could almost feel the presence of the man who had left his indelible mark.

Seth's legacy was entwined with tales of lawlessness and order in the Wild West, a figure who had tamed a wild town amid chaos. It was said his spirit still patrolled the corridors, guarding his creation from the grip of outlaws, both living and not.

In the hotel's dining room, the boys felt an air of anticipation. Shadows seemed to deepen, and the temperature dropped, painting the room in a chilling palette. An unspoken energy enveloped them, like the whispered remnants of long-lost conversations.

From the darkness, a figure emerged—Seth Bullock himself. Solid yet ethereal, he stood as a sentinel, a living embodiment of history. Max and Bryson exchanged wide-eyed glances, transfixed by the sight of the legendary sheriff.

Terrapin's alert ears and watchful gaze mirrored their own curiosity. The atmosphere thickened, as if the air itself bore the weight of the past. A sense of awe and reverence settled upon them, marking the intersection of time and the inexplicable.

Seth's form was a portrait of the Old West—a sturdy frame clad in a worn leather duster, a Stetson perched atop his head, casting his features in shadow. His eyes, deep and knowing, held stories that stretched beyond words. It was as if the essence of a bygone era had taken shape before them.

In the quiet, Seth's gaze swept over the room, as if assessing the safety of his territory. Max and Bryson shivered, feeling the gravity of his presence and the history he represented.

A melancholic air seemed to envelope Seth—a longing, a seeking. It was as if he yearned for acknowledgment, for assurance that his efforts endured. Max and Bryson exchanged a solemn look, recognizing the unspoken plea in the ghostly sheriff's demeanor.

"We understand," Max murmured, addressing the spectral figure. "You did a remarkable job. The hotel remains a sanctuary, and your legacy lives on."

Bryson nodded, his voice carrying a thread of respect. "You can find your rest now, Seth. Your mission is complete, and the Bullock Hotel stands strong."

A glimmer of appreciation danced in Seth's eyes, a smile touching his lips. As if granted solace, his form began to waver, becoming translucent, melding with the room's ambience. The air seemed to warm, carrying a sense of closure and tranquility.

Witnessing the fading presence of Seth Bullock's spirit, Max and Bryson felt a profound connection to the past. In his departure, they felt a bridge between history and the present, a reminder of the enduring spirits that shape the landscapes they traversed.

With a final shimmer, the room reverted to its ordinary state, the echoes of Seth's presence lingering like a whisper. Max and Bryson exchanged a contemplative look, aware of the privilege they'd been granted—a glimpse into a world that existed beyond their own.

Stepping out of the dining room, they stepped into the cool night, carrying with them the weight of the past. The tales of the Old West and the encounters they had experienced melded into a tapestry of memories. Terrapin led the way, her presence a testament to the bond that had formed during their journey.

As they walked under the stars, Max and Bryson knew their South Dakota adventure was ending. The stories of Seth Bullock, the guardian of Deadwood, echoed in their minds. With the wind rustling through the trees and the night alive with secrets, they walked on, ready to carry the legacy of their journey with them.

Their South Dakota adventure reached its conclusion with a sense of wonder—a tribute to history, the mysterious encounters, and the landscapes that had shaped their path. With the knowledge that the past was an integral part of their journey, they ventured onward, ready to embrace new horizons and the stories that awaited in the chapters yet to come.

Conclusion: Embracing the Mysteries of South Dakota

In the heart of South Dakota, Max, Bryson, and Terrapin embarked on an adventure that delved into the very fabric of history. From the Corn Palace's vibrant murals to the mysterious echoes of Sica Hollow, each chapter added a layer to their understanding of this intriguing state.

Their path had been guided by the journal they unearthed at Cypress Manor during their first escapade in "Louisiana's Ghostly Gumbo." With each page they turned, their connection to the past grew stronger, and the whispers of the journal now pointed them towards the Lone Star State, Texas.

As they stood beneath South Dakota's expansive sky, its vastness seemed to mirror the endless possibilities that lay before them. The Black Hills held tales of spectral guardians and haunted histories, while the Bullock Hotel's lingering presence left an indelible mark on their souls.

With the lingering echoes of Seth Bullock's legacy and the lady in white's melancholic gaze, Max, Bryson, and Terrapin felt a deep reverence for the stories that shaped the state. Their journey through South Dakota had brought them face to face with history's mysteries, reminding them that the past was a treasure trove waiting to be unlocked.

As the stars twinkled above, casting their glow upon the rolling landscapes, the trio couldn't help but feel a mixture of excitement and nostalgia. Their steps had left imprints on the paths of history, and as they looked towards Texas—the Lone Star State—they carried the echoes of South Dakota with them.

The journal's pages whispered of new adventures, promising riddles to solve and tales to uncover. With history as their guide and curiosity as their compass, they were prepared to embark on yet another chapter, weaving their own stories into the rich tapestry of the Lone Star State.

The chapters of their journey were far from over; the whispers of the unknown would continue to beckon. And as they bid farewell to South Dakota, they embraced the winding road ahead, ready to unravel more mysteries and discover the hidden gems that awaited them.

The End

Made in the USA
Las Vegas, NV
30 August 2023

76852322R00042